This book belongs to:

....

This book was written for each and every child who is fascinated by trains. May you never lose your sense of excitement, joy and wonder.

If you enjoy this book, please consider leaving a review. I am an independent author and this helps me tremendously. Thank you!

Trains zoom past!

They click and they clack
as they run on the track.

Up the hill...

and back down low.

Coast to coast,
to and fro.

Trains can be old.

Trains can be new.

They can be yellow,

green,

red

or blue.

Over bridges...

through tunnels they go.

Some go fast, some go slow.

Choo Choo Choo

WHOOOSH!

The engine pulls the carriages along.

It is so powerful and strong!

Some trains carry passengers.

Others carry freight - metal, coal, wood - things heavy in weight.

This one has two carriages.

This one has four.

This one has six.

This one has more!

"All change please!" I hear the conductor shout, as all the passengers flood out.

Trains arrive at the station once they reach their destination.